Sum of In Pieces

Sally Field

Conversation Starters

By Paul Adams
Book Habits

Please Note: This is an unofficial Conversation Starters guide. If you have not yet read the original work, you can purchase the original book here.

Copyright © 2018 by BookHabits. All Rights Reserved. First Published in the United States of America 2018

We hope you enjoy this complimentary guide from BookHabits. Our mission is to aid readers and reading groups with quality thought-provoking material to in the discovery and discussions on some of today's favorite books.

Disclaimer / Terms of Use: This guide is unofficial and unauthorized. It is not authorized, approved, licensed, or endorsed by the original book's author or publisher and any of their licensees or affiliates. Product names, logos, brands, and other trademarks featured or referred to within this publication are the property of their respective trademark holders and are not affiliated with BookHabits. The publisher and author make no representations or warranties with respect to the accuracy or completeness of these contents and disclaim all warranties such as warranties of fitness for a particular purpose.

No part of this publication may be reproduced or retransmitted, electronic or mechanical, without the written permission of the publisher.

Bonus Downloads
*Get Free Books with **Any Purchase** of Conversation Starters!*

Every purchase comes with a FREE download!

Add spice to any conversation
Never run out of things to say
Spend time with those you love

Get it Now

or Click Here.

Scan Your Phone

Tips for Using Conversation Starters:

EVERY GOOD BOOK CONTAINS A WORLD FAR DEEPER THAN the surface of its pages. Questions herein are designed to bring us beneath the surface of the page and invite us into the world that lives on. These questions can be used to:

- Foster a deeper understanding of the book
- Promote an atmosphere of discussion for groups
- Assist in the study of the book, either individually or corporately
- Explore unseen realms of the book as never seen before

Table of Contents

Introducing *In Pieces* 6
Discussion Questions 15
Introducing the Author 36
Fireside Questions 43
Quiz Questions 54
Quiz Answers 67
Ways to Continue Your Reading 68

Introducing *In Pieces*

In Pieces is a memoir written by award-winning actress Sally Field. The book features the highs and lows of her career as a Hollywood actress and gives readers behind-the-scenes look into her important relationships with her mother, her grandmother and the other women in her family. While the women play significant roles in her life, she reveals her struggles to be respected and acknowledged by the men who drew close to her, including her husbands and the actor Burt Reynolds. She talks about a lonely childhood and her acting vocation that enabled her to express herself. The book also reveals her most heart-breaking moments including the molestation she suffered in the hands of her stepfather and the realization that her mother knew about it, her abortion at the age of 17, and an eating disorder that came with feelings of loneliness. The book includes the story of how she raised her three sons and how her two marriages eventually led to divorce.

She dedicates the book to her three sons and all of their children. A photo of her mother holding her when she was a baby is shown next to the dedication page. The prologue describes the scene where she first acted in a classroom play as a 12-year-old. She shares her memories of the place, a hospital turned into a classroom, and how she felt playing the role of a girl who turned her back against a boy. The prologue also tells how she started acting in school and how she craved for her mother's approval of her very first stage performance in school.

The first chapter introduces the women who played important roles in her life. Margaret Morlan, her actress-mother is described by her as a beautiful woman who left Field's father when she was three years old. Her grandmother Joy is a woman who, ironically, rarely smiled. It was Joy's presence that created a rock-sturdy strength in Field, though she was not expressive of her love with hugs and kisses. The other women who helped raise her were her grandmother's sister Gladys and their mother, Field's great-grandmother Mimmie. Field tells the story of how these women helped her through her difficult childhood and her years as a young woman faced with challenging life situations which included her acting career. Aside from the theme of women's nurturing presence, Field's story is marked by the theme of men's imposing and controlling presence in her life. The men who got close to her demanded that she play a second role to them and that she give up her own desires and needs in order to please them. One of these men was her stepfather, Jock Mahoney, who repeatedly molested her as a young girl. Field's conflicting feelings about Mahoney is revealed which is typical of women who were abused by somebody they loved. She attempts to excuse his behavior but also questions if his behavior was his way of loving her. The book shows how her childhood and her personality have been fragmented because of this experience. The book's title alludes to the different fragments of her personality that seemed to be in conflict with each other. This influenced and affected her relationships with other men as well as her career. Field tells stories of how she experienced repeated sexual harassment from men in her profession and those she married and loved. The Monkees teased her with humiliating sexual jokes while they filmed the movie "The Flying Nun." Director Bob Rafaelson accordingly suggested she show her naked upper body to him in order to convince him of her getting the role. Actor Burt

Reynolds, who became her boyfriend, did not appreciate her talent and demanded she put him first over her career. Field says she gave in to the demands of the men who put her down. "I eliminated most of me...becoming a familiar, shadowy version of myself..." But she was also brave enough to put a stop to the abusive behavior. When she won the lead role for the movie Norma Rae, Reynolds wanted her to drop it. This time Field fought for it and defended her decision to do the role. She went on to win the Oscar's best actress award. This steely part of Field is seen in the roles she played in the movies but unknown to her fans, it is a characteristic that she did not always perform in real life. She played strong women characters in the films Places in the Heart, Steel Magnolias, Absence of Malice, and Mrs. Doubtfire. Her honesty in writing about herself is shown in the book. Cited by critics for its "raw honesty and pitch-perfect prose" told in a first-person voice, she acknowledges that she was not always present in her sons' lives and that she was not always patient with her mother who helped her take care of her sons. The book provides numerous black and white faded photos of Field as a baby, a toddler, her childhood years with her siblings and family.

Booklist's review says Field writes in a "soulful, wryly witty, and lyrical" manner. She is also cited for courage and honesty. The book shows the experiences that provided her the source for her deeply felt and empathic performances. The review says these lie behind her being a "powerful artist." *USA Today* says the memoir is shocking in its frankness which is rare among celebrities who write their memoirs. *The New York Times Book Review* says the book is outstanding in its "clarity and grace." It tells readers not to expect a Sally Field who is "plucky and desperate to be liked." Field is praised for her courageous "act of personal investigation." The *Atlantic Journal-Consitution* review says Field shows her vulnerable side. It is "the opposite of a self-aggrandizing, celebrity biography…" The New York Magazine review says the memoir is "a classic in the making." It predicts the book's long-lasting effect in the field of memoir publishing.

In Pieces is written by Field who won three Emmy and two Oscar awards. She is known for her roles in the films Norma Rae and Steel Magnolias. She was inducted into the American Academy of Arts and Sciences in 2012 and is a 2015 National Medal of Arts awardee.

Discussion Questions

"Get Ready to Enter a New World"

Tip: Begin with questions dealing with broader issues to ensure ample time for quality discussions. Read through all discussion questions before engaging.

~~~

question 1

The prologue describes the scene where she first acted in a classroom play as a 12-year-old. She shares her memories of the place, a hospital turned into a classroom, and how she felt playing the role of a girl who turned her back against a boy. How does she describe the classroom? How did she feel during the time she was acting?

~~~

~~~

question 2

The prologue also tells how she started acting in school and how she craved for her mother's approval of her very first stage performance in school. How did her mother react when she saw Field's first stage performance? How did Field feel toward her mother's reaction?

~~~

~~~

question 3

The first chapter introduces the women who played important roles in her life. Margaret Morlan, her actress-mother is described by her as a beautiful woman who left Field's father when she was three years old. How else does she describe her mother?

~~~

~~~

question 4

Her grandmother Joy is a woman who, ironically, rarely smiled. It was Joy's presence that created a rock-sturdy strength in Field, though she was not expressive of her love with hugs and kisses. How did Joy support her through Field's difficult times?

~~~

~~~

question 5

The other women who helped raise her were her grandmother's sister Gladys and their mother, Field's great-grandmother Mimmie. How does she describe these women? What kind of lives did they have when they were younger?

~~~

~~~

question 6

Aside from the theme of women's nurturing presence, Field's story is marked by the theme of men's imposing and controlling presence in her life. The men who got close to her demanded that she play a second role to them and that she give up her own desires and needs in order to please them. Who were these men? How did they control her life?

~~~

~~~

question 7

Jock Mahoney repeatedly molested her as a young girl. Field's conflicting feelings about Mahoney is revealed which is typical of women who were abused by somebody they loved. How did she feel about him?

~~~

~~~

question 8

The book shows how her childhood and her personality have been fragmented because of this experience. The book's title alludes to the different fragments of her personality that seemed to be in conflict with each other. How did the fragmentation show in her life?

~~~

~~~

question 9

Field tells stories of how she experienced repeated sexual harassment from men in her profession and those she married and loved. What stories did she tell about the sexual harassment?

~~~

~~~

question 10

Field says she gave in to the demands of the men who put her down. "I eliminated most of me…becoming a familiar, shadowy version of myself…" Can you cite instances of her being her shadowy version of herself?

~~~

~~~

question 11

The steely part of Field is seen in the roles she played in the movies but unknown to her fans, it is a characteristic that she did not always perform in real life. She played strong women characters in the films Places in the Heart, Steel Magnolias, Absence of Malice, and Mrs. Doubtfire. Which of these movies do you see her in her strongest female character? How did she show her strength?

~~~

~~~

question 12

Her honesty in writing about herself is shown in the book. The book is cited by critics for its "raw honesty and pitch-perfect prose" told in a first-person voice. What are the unflattering sides to her character? How does she write about these?

~~~

~~~

question 13

The book provides numerous black and white faded photos of Field as a baby, a toddler, her childhood years with her siblings and family. How does she use these photos to elaborate on her childhood and family stories? Which photo intrigues you most why?

~~~

~~~

question 14

When she won the lead role for the movie Norma Rae, Reynolds wanted her to drop it. This time Field fought for it and defended her decision to do the role. She went on to win the Oscar's best actress award. How did Reynolds regard her acting career compared to his?

~~~

~~~

question 15

She reveals an eating disorder she had that came along with feelings of loneliness. She also talks about a lonely childhood and her acting vocation that enabled her to express herself. How did her acting craft help her cope with loneliness? How did it help her express herself?

~~~

~~~

question 16

Booklist's review says Field writes in a "soulful, wryly witty, and lyrical" manner. She is also cited for courage and honesty. The book shows the experiences that provided her the source for her deeply felt and empathic performances. The review says these lie behind her being a "powerful artist." Can you cite parts of the book which shows her wryly witty voice? How does this affect the soulful and lyrical parts in the book?

~~~

~~~

question 17

USA Today says the memoir is shocking in its frankness which is rare among celebrities who write their memoirs. Which celebrity memoir is written in contrast to Field's frankness? What makes her book shocking? Why?

~~~

~~~

question 18

The New York Times Book Review says the book is outstanding in its "clarity and grace." It tells readers not to expect a Sally Field who is "plucky and desperate to be liked." Field is praised for her courageous "act of personal investigation." Where in the book do you think exemplifies Field's clarity and grace? In what way do the clarity and grace show?

~~~

~~~

question 19

The Atlantic Journal-Constitution review says Field shows her vulnerable side. It is "the opposite of a self-aggrandizing, celebrity biography…" How do you feel reading about her vulnerabilities?

~~~

~~~

question 20

The New York Magazine review says the memoir is "a classic in the making." It predicts the book's long-lasting effect in the field of memoir publishing. Do you agree? Why? Why not?

~~~

Introducing the Author

Sally Field is a multi-awarded actress, having won two Oscars, three Emmies, two Golden Globes, a Screen Actors Guild, a Tony nominee, and two BAFTAs. She started as a television actress in 1965 in the sitcom *Gidget* where she played the lead role. This was followed by *The Flying Nun* in 1967 and *The Girl with Something Extra* in 1973. In 1976, she played the lead role in the TV miniseries *Sybi*l which launched her acting career into a higher level. Her portrayal of Sybil, a woman with a multiple personality disorder won her an Emmy Award as a lead actress. She made several significant movies in the 70s. It was in the late 70s and early 80s that she made the movies that won her the Academy Awards for Best Actress. The first of these is in the 1979 movie *Norma Rae* where she played a labor union leader. Her second Oscar was as the lead actress in the 1984 movie *Places in the Heart*. She made many more critically acclaimed and top-grossing films in the following years, including *Steel Magnolias* in 1989, *Mrs. Doubtfire* in 1993, and *Forrest Gump* in 1994. The 2000s saw her doing the TV series *ER*, which won her another Emmy Award, and *Brothers and Sisters* for which she won her third Emmy Award. She played the character of Aunt May in 2012 *The Amazing Spider-Man* film and its sequel in 2014.

The field has directed the 1996 film *The Christmas Tree*, an episode in the miniseries *From Earth to the Moon* which was shown on HBO in 1998, and the 2000 feature film *Beautiful*.

Field studied acting with Lee Strasberg who became her mentor. Through his guidance, she was able to evolve from her TV image as the girl next door and on to her first major role that won her recognition, *Sybil*.

She wrote her memoir in a span of six to seven years. Before writing the book, she thought she had no voice, but she said something in her was wanting to be said. " I could hardly breathe and I couldn't settle down," she said, describing the feeling of needing to write. She especially felt its urgency when her mother died. In her book, she writes about her strongly felt need to be with her mother as a child. In the first chapter, she talks of her desire to be with her mother even now that she is an adult. 'I wait for my mother to haunt me as she promised she would...," she says. She says her waiting for her is not new because as early as she was five years old, she remembers waiting for her mother to come to fetch her from the school where she just had another panic attack. Her mother is Margaret Morlan, a "drop-your-jaw" beautiful woman who had dark chocolate eyes. She remembers the feeling of being lifted "off the ground in an invisible embrace..." when her mother looked at her.

In writing about the time she had an abortion when she was 17, she describes the feeling of being confused and hazy minded as she went through the operation. The operation was a clandestine one and she felt sick and not clear-minded. She remembers wanting to hug her mother as she told her and her stepfather the news that she was pregnant. She felt the resentment that she had to go through her stepfather's arms first before she could reach the comforting arms of her mother. A few weeks after her abortion, she started her first TV show Gidget which featured her in the lead. She says she loved having a father in the show who looked after her and was respectful of her. It was something she did not have in real life. After doing her TV scenes, she would go home to her real unhappy family, the opposite of the happy family she portrayed in the show. Paris' second book, "The Breakdown," tells the story of Cass, a woman who decides to take a shortcut to her home in the middle of a violent thunderstorm. In her way, she spots a woman who crashed her car and needs help, but Cass doesn't stop. The day after, she learns that the woman has been murdered. After those events, Cass starts feeling guilty and forgetting everyday normal things, like where she left her car, or if she took her pills.

Bonus Downloads

*Get Free Books with **Any Purchase** of Conversation Starters!*

Every purchase comes with a FREE download!

Add spice to any conversation
Never run out of things to say
Spend time with those you love

Get it Now

or Click Here.

Scan Your Phone

Fireside Questions

"What would you do?"

Tip: These questions can be a fun exercise as it spurs creativity among the readers by allowing alternate scene endings and "if this was you" questions.

~~~

question 21

In 1976, she played the lead role in the TV miniseries Sybil which launched her acting career into a higher level. Her portrayal of Sybil, a woman with a multiple personality disorder won her an Emmy Award as a lead actress. How does the Sybil story reflect the title of her memoir? What do you think about the semblance?

~~~

~~~

question 22

It was in the late 70s and early 80s that she made the movies that won her the Academy Awards for Best Actress. The first of these is in the 1979 movie Norma Rae where she played a labor union leader. What is significant about the character of Norma Rae? How does this reflect her real-life character?

~~~

~~~

question 23

She wrote her memoir in a span of six to seven years. Before writing the book, she thought she had no voice, but she said something in her was wanting to be said. How did she feel about the need to write the memoir?

~~~

~~~

question 24

In her book, she writes about her strongly felt need to be with her mother as a child. In the first chapter, she talks of her desire to be with her mother even now that she is an adult. 'I wait for my mother to haunt me as she promised she would...," she says. She says her waiting for her is not new because as early as she was five years old, she remembers waiting for her mother to come to fetch her from the school where she just had another panic attack. What does this say of her relationship with her mother? Were they always close?

~~~

~~~

question 25

In the TV show Gidget, she says she loved having a father who looked after her and was respectful of her. It was something she did not have in real life. After doing her scenes, she would go home to her real unhappy family, the opposite of the happy family she portrayed in the show. How does this story make you feel? What does it tell you about artists and their real lives as opposed to their screen lives?

~~~

~~~

question 26

The book shows the difficult experiences that provided her the source for her deeply felt and empathic performances. These lie behind her being a "powerful artist." If she was not abused by her stepfather, do you think she would be a powerful artist? Why? Why not?

~~~

~~~

question 27

The Atlantic Journal-Constitution review says Field shows her vulnerable side. It is "the opposite of a self-aggrandizing, celebrity biography…" If she did not show her vulnerable side, how would the book be like? Will it be as well-liked by critics?

~~~

~~~

question 28

When she won the lead role for the movie Norma Rae, Reynolds wanted her to drop it. Field fought for it and defended her decision to do the role. She went on to win the Oscar's best actress award. If she did not stand against Reynolds, would her career be as successful as today? Why? Why not?

~~~

~ ~ ~

question 29

She wrote her memoir in a span of six to seven years. Before writing the book, she thought she had no voice, but she said something in her was wanting to be said. " I could hardly breathe and I couldn't settle down," she said, describing the feeling of needing to write. She especially felt its urgency when her mother died. If she decided not to write the book, what would it be the effect on her?

~ ~ ~

~~~

question 30

Field directed the 1996 film The Christmas Tree, an episode in the miniseries From Earth to the Moon which was shown on HBO in 1998, and the 2000 feature film Beautiful. If she focused more on directing films, do you think she would be a successful director? Why? Why not?

~~~

Quiz Questions

"Ready to Announce the Winners?"

Tip: Create a leaderboard and track scores to see who gets the most correct answers. Winners required. Prizes optional.

~~~

quiz question 1

Her actress-mother, _____, is described by her as a beautiful woman who left Field's father when she was three years old.

~~~

~~~

quiz question 2

Her grandmother ____ is a woman who, ironically, rarely smiled. It was her grandmother's presence that created a rock-sturdy strength in Field, though she was not expressive of her love with hugs and kisses.

~~~

~~~

quiz question 3

Actor _____ who became her boyfriend, did not appreciate her talent and demanded she put him first over her career.

~~~

~~~

quiz question 4

True or False: Field says she gave in to the demands of the men who put her down. "I eliminated most of me…becoming a familiar, shadowy version of myself…" she said.

~~~

~ ~ ~

quiz question 5

True or False: Field tells the story of how the women in her family helped her through her difficult childhood and her years as a young woman faced with challenging life situations which included her acting career.

~ ~ ~

~~~

quiz question 6

True or False: The prologue also tells how she started acting in school and how she craved for her father's approval of her very first stage performance in school.

~~~

~~~

quiz question 7

True or False: The book's title alludes to the different fragments of her personality that seemed to be in conflict with each other.

~~~

~~~

quiz question 8

Her portrayal of _____, a woman with a multiple personality disorder won her an Emmy Award as a lead actress.

~~~

~~~

quiz question 9

Her second Oscar was as lead actress in the 1984 movie _____.

~~~

~~~

quiz question 10

True or False: The 2000s saw her doing the TV series ER, which won her another Emmy Award, and Brothers and Sisters for which she won her third Emmy Award.

~~~

~~~

quiz question 11

True or False: She played the character of Aunt May in 2012 The Amazing Spider-Man film and its sequel in 2014.

~~~

~~~

quiz question 12

True or False: She wrote her memoir in one year.

~~~

Quiz Answers

1. Margaret Morlan
2. Joy
3. Burt Reynolds
4. True
5. True
6. False
7. True
8. Sybil
9. Places in the Heart.
10. True
11. True
12. False

Ways to Continue Your Reading

EVERY month, our team runs through a wide selection of books to pick the best titles for readers and reading groups, and promotes these titles to our thousands of readers – sometimes with free downloads, sale dates, and additional brochures.

[Click here to sign up for these benefits.](#)

If you have not yet read the original work or would like to read it again, you can purchase the original book here.

Bonus Downloads
*Get Free Books with **Any Purchase** of* Conversation Starters!

Every purchase comes with a FREE download!

Add spice to any conversation
Never run out of things to say
Spend time with those you love

Get it Now

or Click Here.

Scan Your Phone

On the Next Page…

If you found this book helpful to your discussions and rate it a 4 or 5, please write us a review on the next page.

Any length would be fine but we'd appreciate hearing you more! We'd be very encouraged.

Till next time,

BookHabits

"Loving Books is Actually a Habit"

CPSIA information can be obtained
at www.ICGtesting.com
Printed in the USA
BVHW071354150620
581543BV00004B/729